Jade Franks

Eat The Rich
(but maybe not me mates x)

Salamander Street

PLAYS

First published in 2025 by Salamander Street Ltd., a Wordville imprint. (info@salamanderstreetcom).

Eat The Rich (but maybe not me mates x), © Jade Franks, 2025

Cover Photography: Holly Revell

Cover Design: Michael Julings

PB ISBN: 9781068233449

10 9 8 7 6 5 4 3 2 1

Further copies of this publication can be purchased from
www.salamanderstreet.com

Wordville

INTRODUCTION

Jade asked me to write an introduction to her play, like I'm Stephen Fry and she, Jane Austen. But unlike both Jade and Stephen Fry, I did not go to Cambridge, or university at all for that matter. Just like Jane Austen, I went to an all-girls school; however I doubt Austen had the same experience of queuing up for Pasta King and getting bullied for wearing an anti-bullying wristband. My point is, writing a long essay that tells you how clever I am and spoiling the play you're about to read is not really my thing. Instead I thought I'd give you an insight into what it was like working with Jade, through the data collection method closest to my heart: Spotify wrapped.

On 11 different occasions Jade referred to herself as a genius.

17 times she insisted on starting the play again (16 times I managed to talk her down.)

I spent one night at Jade's family home in Liverpool.

We spent nine hours and 58 minutes talking about the play on the phone.

I went to one Cambridge graduation ceremony where I:

—Got shouted at for being too loud.

—Met the nicest lady who was the wife of the Master of Jade's college.

—Sat through an hour-long assembly in Latin (where a parent sat opposite me winked and then puppeteered a stuffed Hello Kitty teddy to make it look like Hello Kitty was as bored by the ceremony as I was.)

Jade asked me to check if a scene "captured the hearts and minds of the nation" seven times.

We had 37 coffees.

She bought me dinner.

We spent days together, sometimes writing and sometimes chatting.

Getting to work with Jade on this play has been life-affirming (annoyingly so, because she'll absolutely love that.) Jade and I began working on this play as we both got made redundant. I read drafts and listened to Jade joke that we'll be fine once she gets a West-End transfer, a TV contract and we become the rich that need eating—and I know without those things I probably would've stopped working in theatre all together.

Jade is a special writer, she is thoughtful and funny and political, and when you finish reading this play you'll be jealous at how much time I've got to spend talking and thinking about the world with her. And hopefully you know someone who knows someone who can give her a West-End transfer and a TV contract so that I can be rich and problematic too.

I hope you enjoy.

Ellie Fulcher
2025

P.S I wrote this introduction 45-minutes before the publishing deadline (in a Dunelm in Catford), which is very in keeping with how Jade would write drafts for the deadlines I set her for this play. So although it might not encapsulate every thought, feeling and political intent of *Eat The Rich*—it is entirely in keeping with Jade.

THANKS YOUS

Ellie, Jasmyn, Tatenda <3

Roly, Zoe, Lauren, Hannah, Holly, Olly, Michael

The Seven Dials Playhouse and The Unity Theatre

Tommo and The Everyman Theatre Playwrights' Group

Vicky, Milli, Mojola, Sally, Luke, Bobby, Hasan, Dan, Gracie

My angel Justin, who I doubt I'd of made it through uni without.

The many people who donated to the GoFundMe that got us here.

St Edmund's College who also supported the play—restorative justice at its finest.

My mates from home, especially Meg who has sent me upwards of 200 Moonpigs over the years.

The Queens of Flat 3B & the kind mates who have let me crash at theirs after I moved out of London.

To my Mum and Dad who let me come back home so I could get better and feel more me again.

To Tara and Charlie, siblings turned best mates. Sorry you aren't in the play Charl, better luck next time.

And finally, to Dr Jonathan Padley who worked in outreach at Cambridge, got me in and looked after me for three years—if I was a better student, maybe I'd have the words to express how grateful I am that you exist.

The first performance of *Eat The Rich (but maybe not me mates x)* was at Pleasance Courtyard at The Edinburgh Fringe Festival in 2025.

This playtext was sent to print before the end of rehearsals and so some of the text may be different to the performance.

Any resemblance to people, living or dead, or places or actual events are totally coincidental. This is a work of fiction.

Writer & Performer:	**Jade Franks**
Director:	**Tatenda Shamiso**
Producer:	**Jasmyn Fisher-Ryner**
Dramaturg:	**Ellie Fulcher**
Sound Designer:	**Roly Botha**
Lighting Designer:	**Zoe Beeny**
Stage Manager:	**Lauren Lambert Moore**

THE CAST & CREW

Jade | Jade Franks (she/her)

Jade is an actor, writer and director interested in socially engaging and comedic work. She collaborates with venues and producers as an outreach manager to invite audiences who may not otherwise come to the theatre. Jade was previously Education Associate at The Royal Court Theatre and has worked with Open Door, Clean Break and within various prisons on writing projects.

As an actor: *SAGA* (BBC Radio 4), *Hot In Here* (Gate Theatre), *One Night Stand with Felix Mufti* (Royal Court), *Run and Painkiller* (Theatre Royal Stratford East).

As an Outreach Manger: *Hadestown* (Lyric), *Retrograde* (Apollo); *Death of England* (Soho Place); *Hot Wing King* (National Theatre) and *For Black Boys Who Have Considered Suicide When The Hue Gets Too Heavy* (Royal Court & West End).

Assistant Directing credits include: *Liberation Squares* (assisting Milli Bhatia, Brixton House & UK Tour), *Cuckoo* (assisting Vicky Featherstone, Royal Court Theatre.)

Jade is currently on the Playwrights' Programme at the Everyman Theatre in Liverpool.

Director | Tatenda Shamiso (he/him)

Tatenda is a director, writer, dramaturg and performance maker with origins from Zimbabwe, Belgium, the United States and Switzerland. He is an Arts Foundation Fellow in Theatre Writing, and received the 2023 Evening Standard Theatre Award in Emerging Talent for his solo show *NO I.D.* (Royal Court Theatre). Website: tatendashamiso.com

As a director: *1884* (Shoreditch Town Hall), *Housewarming* (Theatre Peckham), as writer/performer: *NO I.D.* (Royal Court/VAULT Festival/Theatre Peckham) and as performer: *Sundown Kiki Reloaded* (Young Vic.)

Associate Director credits includes: *A Good House* (The Royal Court & Bristol Old Vic), *For Black Boys Who Have Considered Suicide When The Hue Gets Too Heavy* (West End), *Choir Boy* (Bristol Old Vic.)

Assistant Director credits includes: *Wolves on the Road* (Bush Theatre), *A Streetcar Named Desire* (Almedia & West End), *Bootycandy* (Gate Theatre.)

Producer | Jasmyn Fisher-Ryner (she/her)

Jasmyn Fisher-Ryner is a two-time Olivier Award-nominated Producer and the founder of JFR Productions, an independent theatre and digital production company based in East London. With a background in both subsidised and commercial theatre, she is known for producing bold, socially conscious work that platforms emerging artists and centres accessibility, representation and radical change.

She was nominated for Best Producer at the Black British Theatre Awards 2022 for her work on *For Black Boys Who Have Considered Suicide When The Hue Gets Too Heavy* (Garrick Theatre 2024, Apollo Theatre 2023, Royal Court Theatre 2022). Jasmyn also produced the Olivier-nominated *Blue Mist* (Royal Court Theatre, 2023) and was Associate Producer on *Why A Black Woman Will Never Be Prime Minister* (Camden People's Theatre, 2024.)

Her practice spans theatre, digital media, events and outreach with a strong focus on collaboration with young people and communities. As a digital producer, she produces and manages the *Frame of Mind* podcast, and as an Events Consultant, she works with the Royal Central School of Speech and Drama.

She previously worked as a producer for the Royal Court Theatre, and currently serves as a Trustee at Hackney Empire.

Dramaturg | Ellie Fulcher (she/her)

Ellie is a freelance dramaturg and writer from South East London. During her time as Literary and Participation Associate at the Royal Court she worked dramaturgically on shows such as *Word-Play* by Rabiah Hussain, *Blue Mist* by Mohamed-Zain Dada, and *Imposter 21* by Molly Davies. Other credits include *Why a Black Woman Will Never Be Prime Minister* by Zakiyyah Deen and *Village Idiot* by Samson Hawkins. Ellie works on writer development programmes with organisations such as Hackney Empire and has dramaturged Hackney Empire's annual artist development programme for the past three years.

Sound Designer | Roly Botha (they/them)

Roly is a theatremaker, composer/sound designer and performer, and Associate Artist of The PappyShow.

Theatre includes: *Uncanny: Fear of the Dark* (Tour); *Letters From Max* (Hampstead); *Playfight* (Soho/Bristol Old Vic/Roundabout); *Gunter* (Royal Court); *Shut Up I'm Dreaming* (National Theatre/Tour); *Dear Young Monster* (Soho/Bristol Old Vic); *BOYS* (Barbican/Southbank Centre/ tour); *Milk & Gall* (Theatre503.)

As music producer/orchestrator includes: *Diary Of A Gay Disaster* (Underbelly/Arcola, WhatsOnStage award for Best Studio Production.)

As associate sound designer includes: *4:48 Psychosis* (Royal Court/RSC); *ECHO* (Royal Court/World Tour); *Cinderella* (Theatre Royal Stratford East.)

Lighting Designer | Zoe Beeny (they/them)

Zoe Beeny is a Lighting Technician and Designer. After completing their degree in Drama and English at Goldsmiths, University of London, they have gone on to work as a technician at The Bridge Theatre and The National Theatre.

Stage Manager | Lauren Lambert Moore (she/her)

Lauren is a director, stage manager and theatre maker—working predominantly on new writing and devised theatre from female and queer voices.

Lauren trained at Central Saint Martins, East 15 Acting School and the National Youth Theatre.

Full credits and testimonials available on Lauren's website laurenlambertmoore.com

JFR Productions

JFR Productions (JFRP) is a multifaceted production company dedicated to crafting moments and cultivating stories through theatrical, event consultancy and digital management.

We are committed to the journey that starts from a passing thought into a fully executed production. Ensuring that all work is accessible and available to all cultures and communities to experience. Because why should anything be gate-kept!

JFRP produces and invests in a range of work that focuses on underrepresented stories and storytelling, through our theatre strand; produces and consults on impactful and meaningful events. The digital element of the company supports producing content that provides a platform for people to discuss topics close to their heart.

jfrproductions.com

Jade Franks

Eat The Rich
(but maybe not me mates x)

CHARACTERS

JADE

20 years old, Scouse

NOTES ON PLAYTEXT

JADE: Lines in this format are when Jade talks to the audience.

JADE: **Lines in this format are Jade in the past tense.**

CHARACTER: *Lines in this format are in the voice of whichever character is speaking.*

The bits where Jade speaks about the future should feel like the pure embodiment of anxiety. They are labelled BIT 1, BIT 2 and BIT 3 for clarity. They run on a separate backwards timeline to the rest of the play.

BIT 3 should feel like it bleeds out of the play, perhaps changing to reference the present day and location of the performance.

SCENE ONE

Choral music in the distance gets closer and closer until it is interrupted by a sudden beep and...

JADE: **Hello you're through to Jade. How can I help?**

JADE: Before my life irreversibly changed forever, I worked in a call centre. And it was sound but I couldn't shake the feeling that I was destined for much greater things.

Don't get me wrong, I wasn't unhappy. But growing up I always had big dreams of Making It. In what I wasn't sure. But I'd struck the perfect balance of having mates, going out, and also bein a massive nerd. And that seemed like the blueprint to success.

I started working in the call centre after not getting into uni, cos even though my final grades were good, my predicted grades were low because I wrote in blue pen in my mocks so got disqualified.

That and Mr Smythe kicked me out of Gifted and Talented cos I put up a story saying he had a head like the Radio City Tower.

Time would go very slowly in that place so I liked to build character profiles of the miserable callers we would get. I'd write short stories and multiverses where the callers would have these mad crossover plots. I'd created a whole Call Centre Cinematic Universe.

My favourite colleague was Denise, she worked in the call centre cafe, and she had the biggest heart.

DENISE: *Look ere chick, I'm not bein funny, ave said it before an I'll say it again, you'd love our baby.*

JADE: **How old's your baby?**

DENISE: *About your age.*

JADE: There is this phenomenon in Liverpool where the youngest of a generation will forever be Our Baby. And if Our Baby has a baby, yes, that baby then becomes Our Baby's Baby.

DENISE: *He was meant to play for Everton yeno, before he got his knee injury.*

JADE: A classic tale, as old as time itself. I had no interest in Our Baby. But I loved listening to Denise's stories. And her daily inspirational quotes.

DENISE: *"You have within you, right now, everything you need to deal with whatever the world can throw at you."*

JADE: Me and the people on my row would play this game called Dickhead Bingo. For a full house the caller must:

1. ask for the manager

2. say something derogatory about Liverpool and

3. call you stupid.

We had found, from our empirical research, that during the summer months it was much harder. I reckon it had something to do with the Premier League being over.

JADE: **Before we continue I must take you through some security questions.**

Well, if you don't answer them I can't verify your identity.

No, I'm afraid I can't escalate this to my manager.

ONE–

Dead busy up here at the moment.

Yeah, that's right, "up here"—the office is in Liverpool... And why do you think it's crazy to base a call center for a pension company in Liverpool? BECAUSE YOU DONT TRUST SCOUSERS WITH YOUR MONEY?!

TWO–

That's a less than kind thing to say, Mr Worthington. I'll have you know we take good care of your fund. No, I don't have a degree in finance. I can assure you though, I am one of the finest minds of this generation. You DISAGREE? And why is that..... Because you think I'm stupid!!

THREE–

JADE: It really wasn't that deep but he starts kickin off being proper nasty saying that I'll never amount to anything and sayin I'm so stupid, blah blah blah, so I go...

JADE: **Well, actually Mr Worthington. I've just got into Oxbridge so I'm not stupid.**

JADE: He tells me Oxbridge isn't actually a place but rather a term used for Oxford and Cambridge collectively.

JADE: **Well, yeah the second one then. I'm going to Cambridge.**

JADE: He asked me what college, I said...

JADE: **The big one ;)**

JADE: When I tell you how this man's attitude switched up. I couldn't believe it. He was so kind to me, retracted his complaint and said he would even write to head office to suggest I get a raise. He wished me all the best and hung up.

Obviously this was a lie but I couldn't stop thinking about it. I spent so long looking on the Cambridge website. The website was brimming with prospective alternative versions of future me. I could be ANYONE. Did you know Olympians go this uni NOBEL PRIZE WINNERS, actors, Politicians, Winners of Tipping Point?!

So, I took myself for the first time down from Cambridge Railway Station along the streets of this unfamiliar town. I walk myself down the cobbled streets with skinny alleyways that were full of secrets and down past the river and the pubs that charge £27 for fish and chips, I thought, if it looks this good on Google street view. I'm gonna have to apply.

I spent the next months working harder than I ever have on a personal statement and reading as much as I could. I got a taste of how nice people like Mr Worthington are to you if you say you go to Cambridge. And I didn't want to let that feeling go.

My sister Laura offered to help practice for my interview. She's a makeup artist and the most glamorous person alive. She works in Boots, and after school I used to go and she'd do my make up while a flock of young women in big hair rollers fought over the fake eyelashes. Scouse Women are like swans. Beautiful—but don't fuck with them.

LAURA: *Which one?*

JADE: **I dunno it's a hard question!**

LAURA: *You have to pick. You can't take this much time in the real thing.*

JADE: **Fine. Shakespeare. Final Answer.**

LAURA: *You'd fuck Shakespeare?!*

JADE: **Yes, and marry Austen. And kill JK Rowling.**

JADE: I can't say anything we practiced came up in the actual interview. But I gave it my best shot.

JADE: **Hello, you're through to Jade. How can I help?**

JADE: I started to think it was all just a silly idea.

JADE: **Yeah and can I just take your name and date of birth?**

JADE: I was constantly refreshing my emails in work.

JADE: **NAME AND DATE OF BIRTH.**

JADE: Until one morning...

JADE: **I'm not bein funny, I can't say it any clearer.**

JADE: I got an email...

JADE: **Fuck me sideways.. sorry sir, no, not you..**

JADE: I hung up and I ran down Old Hall Street, past the town hall and that nice Italian on the corner. I kept running, like Forrest Gump in a blouse and ballet flats.

And I could have kept goin, but I was really out of breath and I remembered it was ages yet before I'd start. So I headed back to tell Denise the good news.

DENISE: *I'm so prouda you girl. Remember: "We can't become what we need to be by remaining what we are."*

JADE: **Nice one, Denise.**

SCENE 2

JADE: The summer went by dead quick and I moved down a few weeks before term started. The colleges where you live don't usually let students back early, but they said it was OK because I'm from a broken home. I'm not, but who was I to question their assumption when there are perks involved

It turned out, Cambridge wasn't a cool place in the south—like Thorpe Park. There's only two Greggs here, Liverpool has 23.

I got a job as a cleaner—easy enough and decent pay. And a good way to meet new people.

I was paired up with a woman called Krystyna. She wasn't very chatty at first. I thought it was because of the language barrier but I soon found out her English is better than mine, she just didn't want to talk to me.

Me and Krystyna spent whole days together cleaning rooms for the incoming students. I would cycle to the big yellow storage unit where she would be waiting in her Ford people carrier and we would load her car with supplies. The smell of the bleach and cleaning products would overpower that family-car smell of old snacks that had been left under a child-seat and mud from the local park and we'd sit, listening to the radio.

Dua Lipa's 'One Kiss' starts to play.

JADE: I see Krystyna's head start bobbing along. So I start bobbin too.

JADE: **Do you like Dua Lipa?!**

JADE: She nods! GET IN.

JADE: **This song was a big reason for Liverpool winning the 2019 Champions League yeno. All the lads at the match would be like :**

One kiss is all it takes

Fallin' in love with me

Possibilities

I look like all you need

JADE: And we BOB! Krystyna joins in the chorus and I feel ALIVE.

The radio cuts out and Krystyna gets out of the car without hesitation or pause to reflect on the beautiful breakthrough moment we just shared.

I liked doing these cleans. I would pass time imagining what kind of people would have inhabited these rooms the years previous based on the clues they left behind.

There were Blu Tack marks from where postcards were carefully put up. They were bought from art gallery gift shops that they would spend their weekends in as teenagers, and others were from European cities with names I don't recognise that their parents took them to. And I'd spend hours scrubbing these walls so that the students would get their deposits back from the college. Like my life depended on it.

Krystyna answers a phone call, from her son's nursery, again. He is in a biting phase—I said to her...

JADE: **Don't worry about it, we've all been there. In year 8 I bit Sophie Smithers until she bled because she called me a slag.**

JADE: Krysyna wasn't interested.

JADE: **I don't mind finishing the rest alone if you need to go.**

JADE: Obviously I did mind but I was trying to get her to like me.

When she's gone I play some tunes out of my phone. Joni Mitchell. I liked to pretend I was a heartbroken stay-at-home wife, cleaning the beautiful Victorian house that I shared with a man who doesn't love me.

When I finish cleaning I realise I have all of the stuff to take back to the storage unit and I do not have a car. I loaded up my bike, I had to put the mop on the seat between my legs like the world's worst witch. And I put on my helmet, because some part of me must have wanted to live.

As I cycled past some of the older students who were already back, I couldn't wait to be one of them. To relax in that late summer sun, to get a £7 ice cream and sit on the grass in front of one of the most historic, beautiful buildings in England and just not have to worry.

SCENE 3

JADE: In the pursuit of finding friends I headed to
the Freshers Fair. I tagged along with these girls who
insisted on repeating everything I said back to me in my
accent. Was like having a group of aristocratic parrots
followin me round.

I ask them how they think they're gonna cope juggling
their studies, hobbies and a job and they laugh. They
explain that you can't have a job when you study at
Cambridge—it's against the rules. I felt a twinge of stress.
I can't quit—I've only done a couple of shifts and I don't
wanna let Krystyna down. And I like working! I like
having me own money to treat meself.

Whatever, I thought, I'd seen loads of rule breaking
already, there was a group of third years in my college
who all chipped in for a hot tub and put it in their
dorm. So I figured I'd be sound.

These girls are picking up leaflets of the most random
clubs and I think they're joking.

JADE: **Hahahahha yeah right, Polo Club, good one.**

JADE: Then I realise they're not.

JADE: **... Oh... aww. Good choice yeah.**

JADE: I never really had any hobbies. Politics... maybe.
45 of our 58 Prime Minsters did go to Oxford or
Cambridge and I would look fit in a suit. But I think I
swear too much for that. And I probs wouldn't be able
work with people who are indifferent about genocide.

Think of a hobby, a sport, a political cause and there's probably a society for it. And if there wasn't, it's probably just called something else.

For example The Fascist Club is called The Free Speech Society. Those who hate women having autonomy over their own bodies join Cambridge Pro-Life, and A Support Group for Students who weren't hugged enough as children is called The Cambridge Footlights.

There was a stall dedicated to the justice for survivors of sexual assault at the university and I gathered that it was indicative of the fact that there was a need for it.

Suddenly this small but mighty girl, the most Northern girl I'd ever met, confidently comes up to me and asks:

NORTHERN GAL: *Does any of the following apply to you ?*

   —State School Educated

   —Received Free School Meals

   —First Generation in your family to attend university

   —A Full Cambridge Bursary Recipient

JADE: If people knew I was the first in my family to go uni, one of the first in my school to go Cambridge, without any help, I will be branded a genius. And I don't know if I can handle that pressure.

The group I'm with act like she just asked them for spare change.

I realise it's definitely best if they don't know that stuff. But not for the reasons I was worried about.

They shake their heads at the girl and scurry off. And I do the same.

SCENE 4

JADE: The first day of lectures I go over to the man stood at the front of the hall struggling to transfer his PowerPoint from his USB onto the projector—

JADE: **Sir, is this the right room for first year English?**

CJ: *Yes, but please call me CJ.*

Jade: I had to walk through a 400-year-old courtyard to get here. The man is walking with an ivory cane? Surely he's a 'Sir'?

It's clear that a lot of the people here already know each other. Had I missed some kind of induction? A night out? Is there a group chat I'm not in? I bravely headed over and sat next to a group of girls.

TILLY: *Hi, I'm Tilly,*

MILLY: *I'm Milly,*

JILLY: *I'm Jilly!*

JADE: It was like the three witches of Macbeth if they all shopped at Oliver Bonas.

JADE: **Hiya, I'm Jade.**

JADE: I got out my new Macbook. This was the most money I'd spent on anything. I unzipped my bag, unzipped the laptop briefcase and put it on the desk making sure the screen protector was still intact. Tilly, Milly & Jilly follow suit, but with an air of comfortability. They took out their MacBooks RAW from their flimsy tote bags—no case or nothing!

TILLY: *So what school did you go to?*

JADE: I was confused because there are probably around 25,000 schools in the UK?

HERMES: *Darling, don't answer. It's a filtering process.*

JADE: This fella was handwriting his notes in a leather bound notebook with a pen that looked as if you'd be able to refill the cartridge when it ran out. His name was written on the front of his notebook—Hermes.

JADE: **Ahh, like the delivery service?**

HERMES: *No, like the Olympian Deity, considered herald of the Gods.*

JADE: **I'm named after the woman in the Asda who was at the checkout when my Mum went into labour.**

JADE: He thought this was hilarious, and clicked in appreciation. Brilliant, he's gay—I soon came to learn that posh gay people are much more tolerable than the posh straight people.

JADE: **What did you mean about... Filtering...**

HERMES: *Well it's all about what school you went to. And it's not straight-forward as State School versus Private school.*

There are levels to this. You could go to a good state school and be more IN than someone from a cheap private school. You could be home-schooled by your cool artsy parents and more IN than someone who went to an international school. It's more about the circles. Whose parents have dinner parties. Whose families work in the same industry. Whose parents, grandparents, great grandparents all met in this same university.

JADE: I realised I wasn't IN.

And if there's one thing worse than classism and disparity of wealth in this country, it's FOMO.

SCENE 5

JADE: I'm a couple of weeks into term and I'm just about balancing the cleaning job with all the other shit I have to do. In my first lecture CJ said we should be spending 40 hours a week studying—which I guess is why the job rule is in place. I was starting to get quite overwhelmed. But everyone here has a lot going on.

There's 18-year-olds writing books, founding charities, starting their own businesses. It's like a pressure cooker of perfectionism and exceptionalism and I want to scream from the rooftops, 'Can everyone just ava day off?'

But I don't because I'm late for work.

And by work I mean cleaning the sick in students en suites, and discarding empty Ket baggies off their desks.

Me and Krystyna are getting on like a house on fire. She's so sound, and more than happy to keep my little secret about being a Cambridge student with a job, even if she does now call me Wróg. Which is Polish for 'The Enemy.'

She likes to text me fun facts and GIFs. She had to revise so hard for the Life in the UK test and I love a pub quiz, so together we made quite the team.

KRYSTYNA: *Work 2moz! *gif of cat shooting itself in the head* BTW did u know AQUA has more UK number ones than Led Zeplin??! Crazy.*

JADE: But I don't often reply, and it's not personal. I've barely even replied to anyone from home since starting.

I'm so in Uni mode: Lectures! Laundry! Library! Deliveroo! Another Deliveroo, Another Deliveroo! It's exhausting. I do miss home, but then I remember that my student finance and payslip have dropped so I've been buying the most random shit, I have to call my sister Laura to tell her:

JADE: **I got:**
A bath mat that says GET NAKED!
A fish tank
Sea snails for my fish tank
A pairs of 110s
A cafetiere
Smoked salmon
A weighted blanket
Drugs—but dont tell mum
A large one off donation to Choose Love

JADE: The list went on and Laura doesn't say much, just laughs. Mum and Dad and me brothers are coping without me. The dog misses me. Nothing else has changed. But it feels like a hundred years since I saw them.

I found out that the girls I went to the Freshers Fair with made a group chat without me. They didn't wanna talk about the university ski trip in front of me, they felt too bad that I couldn't afford to go. But I don't know where they heard that? I could afford to go. It's just that I have Ibiza booked for the same weekend.

I'm walking back from a seminar with Hermes, he's such a babe and he invites me to a pre-drinks at his before hitting one of the three clubs in Cambridge.

But I had a shift at 9am the next day with Krystyna. I had two choices—I could NOT be hungover from work tomorrow. Or I could TRY and make some friends.

I decided that in the long run, socialising and at least trying to make some friends would serve me better. And ano it may not seem like it, but I do have friends. They were just 199 miles up the M6.

I wanted to make an effort that night. I'd been going on nights out since I was about 14, so if there's something I know how to do—it's dress up.

I spent the whole afternoon getting ready and scouse Prinny Rammers are blaring. I went on a bit of a Pretty Little Thing haul in preparation for the wild Freshers that never happened so I have a few options.

With a blazer dress I could get away with not wearing a coat out—and since I had not yet discovered that they have cloak rooms in the south.

Hermes was at the college opposite. I nip in to Sainsbury's for some drinks and he had texted and asked me to pick him up some cheese.

I strut out and across the cobbled streets, not too different from Matthew Street or Concert Square—so I can handle it. I can feel people staring at me, probably impressed with my walking.

HERMES: *Jadeyyy! You look stunning though.*

JADE: He was wearing the same clothes I saw him in earlier that day. We passed these big groups of rowdy girls and lads.

HERMES: *Urgh... the drinking socs.*

JADE: Hermes explained to me what these 'secret' drinking societies were. He described them as more hetrosexual than Drag Brunch.

HERMES: *OK, so for girls, if you are deemed pretty enough and cool, you will be asked to come to a pre-drinks to further assess your capacity to be pretty and cool.*

For the boys, their pre-drinks include more intense initiations such as drinking each other's piss, pretending to be homeless for a night, and we all know the story of David Cameron and that unfortunate pig.

You will all meet in a private room above a curry house or kebab shop, and this is where the third-year boys will identify and prey on the first-year girls of their choosing, the term for this is Sharking. You parte in more challenges to further assess your ability to be pretty and cool. You will then all head to the club, leaving the establishment in a much worse way than when you arrived, telling the owner to invoice the society for any damages.

In the club, the boys who were sharking you will likely now kiss you, take you home and have sex with you. You have now secured your place IN the drinking soc as you have proven you can be pretty, cool and willing to have sex with the boys.

JADE: **Fuckin hell, this shit's still going on?**

HERMES: *Yeah, last year a boy burnt a £20 note in front of a homeless man.*

JADE: We went into Hermes' room and it was decorated like nothing else I had ever seen.

Paintings and postcards of naked bodies, even a topless portrait of Hermes himself that he said his cousin gave him for his birthday.

JADE: **Are all these books yours?!**

HERMES: *Well, most are my parents. From the family library.*

JADE: I wonder if my Dad's Steven Gerrard autobiography and my Mum's copy of '50 Shades of Grey' constitutes a family library.

In the adjoining room was where his friends were having drinks. In one hand a trusty bottle of Echo Falls, cos it's more classy than Lambrini. The other hand, the cheese for Hermes.

I walk in and they're playing deafening drum and bass. The room was candle-lit with long red wax sticks in wine bottles dripping purposefully like an art installation. In the middle of the table, there was a cheese board. Now, as these people look up to acknowledge me I realise I may have misunderstood.

JADE: **Hey, I'm Ja..**

JADE: Their eyes are drawn to the Sainsbury's own mozzarella and cheddar pre-grated mix that was clutching for dear life. Hermes kindly took it from my hand and replaced it with a wine glass.

One of the lads snorted as he laughed.

TIZZO: *Hahhah, that's sooo jokes, what's up my G, I'm Tizzo.*

JADE: **That`s a unique name!**

TIZZO: *As soon as I start my internship at JP Morgan this summer I'll go back to using my actual name.*

JADE: Tilly, Milly and Jilly from my course are there too. And this fit second-year, Tizzo's roommate and cousin, called Greg. He's from Kent and went to Eton. AND he plays on the uni's football team.

I'd never fancied a man who tied his jumper round his shoulders before, but I was actually kinda into it.

The girls weren't wearing heels but I wasn't massively bothered by that. You do you casual queens. I was sure everyone else would be dressed up.

Greg sits next to me. He is an engineer so naturally, I strike up a conversation about tunnels.

JADE: **There's a river that cuts through Merseyside and there's a tunnel that goes under the sea bed and you can drive through it but the decline and incline is so subtle that you never even feel like you're under the water.**

JADE: Tizzo, Tilly, Milly and Jilly are whispering and giggling in the corner.

JADE: (*Kindly*) **What you guys laughing at?**

MILLY: *We were just talking about how interesting Liverpool sounds.*

JADE: *Clearly someone's been to the Beatles Museum.*

TILLY: *My Daddy once went to Liverpool for work, and..*

MILLY: *What??*

TILLY: *Noo, I can't say.*

MILLY: *Say!!*

TILLY: *I can't!!*

MILLY: *Can she say, Jade?*

JADE: *Yeah, sure, go on.*

TILLY: *Well, he said it was an awful place and someone tried to steal the tires from his car.*

JADE: **He was probably parked like a cunt and deserved it.**

JADE: Oops. Meant to be in my head.

TILLY: *Probably more that he has a Rolls Royce and no one's ever seen one before.*

JADE: I just smiled and nodded and let her continue to say the most awful shit. I don't get what she meant about the car stuff. Most people at home have blacked out BMWs. And they're well expensive.

Hermes turns off the horrendous music and we all down the last of their drinks. As we are walking out Greg turns to me and goes...

GREG: *Ignore her, she's just jealous.*

JADE: **Of what?**

JADE: And he winks at me. What in the Hugh Grant was that? Consider me charmed. He smells amazing—like his laundry gets taken away and done for him (because it does) and his eyes are beautiful and kind—like he has never felt pain or hardship (because he hasn't.)

SCENE 6

JADE: When we got to the club, they were scanning
IDs and I saw Tizzo's Government name comes up as
Timonthy Harold Baldwin-McGomery and I almost
turned around and went home.

We get in. The cha-cha slide was playing. I get to the
bar and do what I've been conditioned to do. Get a
round in. I got everyone a VK.

It turns out these people were not familiar with the
custom of buying rounds, so now I look like I'm trying
to buy friendship. I go to the dancefloor and a remix of
the 'Lion King Circle of Life' starts playing.

Everyone's having the best time. And I just don't
understand.

This place smells, and looks like a Year 7 disco. 20-year-
olds with ties round their heads. Couples covered in
lipstick from eating each other's faces, cups on the
perimeter of the dance floor full of vomit.

And NO ONE one is dressed up.

I take off my heels because I can no longer bear a
bird's-eye view of this scene.

My fake eyelashes are sticking together as I start to cry
thinking about how much I would rather be at home.
With my friends. Who are actually funny and listen to
good music.

I turn and there's Greg. He asks me if I want to leave,
but not with his words, silently, with his eyes.

I nod and he walks me back. He unknotted the quarter-
zip from the centre of his chest to give to me.

JADE: **I'm not cold.**

JADE: And he put it round me anyway.

As we are walking he points out the college where his parents met and then had their wedding just two years after they graduated.

We walk a little further we stop outside a huge wooden gate which is over 200 years old, I open it with a tiny plastic key card.

GREG: *You look so much better without all that on your face you know, and without those massive things on your feet.*

JADE: I looked down at the heels in my hand that had strutted me through adolescence, through my first night in Liverpool and Manchester, that had me in the Royal A&E after falling down the stairs in BaaBaar, that danced on tables in the social clubs where everyone had their 18ths.

Then he kisses me.

I chuck my heels in a bin outside and we go up the spiral staircase to my room.

SCENE 7

JADE: Last night was like an episode from The Crown
X-Rated. Someone saying naughty things to you in the
Queen's English?! This man should have two titles after
his name: MBE and BDE.

That week we were pretty inseparable. He stayed at
mine every night, partly to get some space from Tizzo,
given they basically share a room but mostly because he
fancied me loads. He invited me to come watch him play
for the uni's footy team. Does that make me a WAG?
We do our sainsbury's shop together and he helps me
pick good wines—they're the bottles with the corks. And
at formal dinners he teaches me what cutlery to use for
what course—you start from the outside and work your
way in.

He also just knows everyone and so I slotted right into
his friendship group, which was really nice.

We went out after the match and I wake up, hungover
as fuck, to my phone going off.

JADE: **SHIT, Krystyna, yeah no worries I'm on my way
I'm just leaving now, yeah.**

JADE: I'd forgotten all about work. Greg is not waking
up. I'll just leave him here.

I must have apologised to Krystyna a million times, she
doesn't even care, says she's glad I'm out making friends.

We move on to the next room. And the next, and
the next. Greg texts me 'Morning Beautiful. Just left
yours—I will see you later.' We are finally on the last
room of the shift. We go in and there's a lad asleep,

snoring SO loud in what seems to me like a living room. It's one of those weird adjoining rooms.

Oh No. I get a closer look and it's Tizzo. He stays asleep.

JADE: **Psst, Krystyna, I need to get out of here.**

JADE: She's busy cleaning sleeping beauty's skid marks in the toilet. I can hear footsteps outside the door. And the room is closing in and it feels like someone's cupping the sound around my ears with their hands and I can't really breathe.

And in comes Greg.

BIT 1

My body is like frozen in this state but my mind was racing through time and I thought I could see the future? Like in a few months we could get together and stay together and then I'm at mine and Greg's wedding, and it's intimate and quietly lavish and only a year or so after we graduate. It's in one of the Cambridge gardens. We invite all our old university friends and our family, but it's mostly his family. I dunno where my Dad is and not even Laura's here and we have a pact to be each other's bridesmaids. And my name is double-barrelled. And we would honeymoon in Greg's family's holiday home like Bella and Edward in Twilight Breaking Dawn: Part One. By the time we are home I'm pregnant. I phone my Mum and Dad to tell them and they're buzzing—they're dying to be grandparents. But it's quite a long way to come down south to visit and their health isn't great so they can't drive and the trains are £300. So I ask Greg if he would consider moving up north. He laughs. My Mum and Dad never see the baby, who we call Bartholomew. I read him baby books with Greg's Mum and she corrects my vowels and says she hopes my accent won't confuse him. I realise my baby is nothing like me but it's too late. He supports Arsenal and goes to a school where you have to wear a hat and grows up to be a Lib Dem.

GREG: *Jade? What are you doing here?*

JADE: **Hey! Hi! Yeah I'm just..**

GREG: *Oh God, I'm so sorry the place is a mess, the help is just tidying.*

JADE: **The HELP?**

GREG: *(kindly, to KRYSTYNA)* *Sorry, could you come back later? Thank you so much. (To JADE) Why do you have them gloves on?̱*

JADE: **Oh, er....**

GREG: Were you... Cleaning my room?

JADE: **Ah... yes?**

GREG: *This is why I like you. You're so generous for helping her out. These people are on minimum wage. Remind me to give her a tip at Christmas.*

JADE: And he leans in for a kiss. Krystyna thanks me for my help and takes the gloves off me. Greg didn't question how I knew this was his room or how I got in. He isn't the sharpest tool in the box. But he is fit.

I text Krystyna—thank you for covering for me!! She replied no worries ;) and a GIF of a woman making it rain with dollar bills.

SCENE 8

JADE: After that incident, Krystyna said she would clean
Greg's block alone for the rest of term if I babysat for her
on Tuesdays. Her son's name is Tom and he's really into
slime and mild acts of violence.

The more mates I was making the riskier this double
life was. I didn't wanna risk anyone snitching to the
professors. Grass central, this place.

And I did not need any more eyes on me. It was already
abundantly clear to my professors that I was very behind
on account of not knowing any Latin—they said it
wouldn't matter when I applied.

I was so lost in lectures, it was like treading water.
Sparkling water. For hours and hours.

The uni's solution to this was to pay for me to be tested
for Dyslexia, which was the only test I passed that term.
As part of this test they ask you about your childhood.

SUE: *And in school, were you a late developer?*

JADE: **OMG, yeah I didn't get tits till I was aba 18.**

BIT 2

It's happening again. The room closing in and it sounds
like a goldfish bowl is round my head.

I'm imagining my third year doing my dissertation and
while Hermes is getting feedback from his parents,
corrections and suggestions of books and academics
to cite. I go home and Laura takes the piss out of my
outfit so I call her outfit chavvy. I argue with my Mum

an Dad cos I'm just frustrated that they don't get what it's like for me and rather than asking tutors for extra help, I use big words that sound patronising and make people feel small and everyone at home collectively tells me to 'fuck off back to Cambridge.' So I do. Forever. And I stay there after I graduate and that's when Greg asks me to marry him and we get married in the college gardens and it's intimate and quietly lavish...

SUE: *Jade?*

JADE: **Yeah, sorry.**

JADE: I then had to go to a lot of meetings with that same really well-meaning lady called Sue who truly believed the answer to all my problems could be solved with yellow paper and the Pomodoro Technique.

SUE: *My darling, my darling, my darling, you see you just need to tap into a more growth mindset. Remember: "We can't become what we need to be by remaining what we are."*

JADE: If Denise from the call centre didn't have Our Baby so young, and didn't have to bring him up on her own and work in that cafe, I wondered if she could be paid £100 an hour like Sue is.

The uni also gave me a printer and an iPad to help me, but I felt bad taking them. Like I didn't earn it.

SUE: *Don't dwell on things so much. You should make lists of things you are looking forward to!*

JADE: So I gave it a go.

1. I'm going on a date with Greg to the Ivy for our one-month anniversary.

2. Krystyna's invited me to her kid's birthday party.

3. Laura is coming to visit today.

Greg is stressed because Laura arrives at four and he can't find his nice watch.

JADE: **I haven't seen you with that for ages! And tbh, unless it's a diamond-encrusted Rolex, Laura's not gonna notice it or care that you have it on.**

JADE: Laura's Uber pulled up outside my college.

She ran over and gave me the biggest hug. We never really hugged growing up but in that moment it felt like whatever the reverse of the big bang would be. Everything came back together and felt tiny, close and alright again.

LAURA: *Fuckin hell Jade this place is mental.*

JADE: She's looking around in awe of the place. And something within me cringes, I dunno like, second-hand embarrassment by how amazed she is by it all.

The porters of the colleges are like the gatekeepers of hell. They'd be hunched over the desks at the entrances of the college ready to turn away any student who didn't 'seem' like they belong here.

For instance, most of Hermes' family are East-Asian and when they came to visit the porters wouldn't let them in cos they thought they were tourists, despite him showing his own Cambridge University card.

At least I could change how I spoke.

JADE: **Just keep your voice down when we go in yeah? Just walk straight through don't say nothin.**

LAURA: (*Loudly*) *Iya mate, lovely hat.*

PORTER: *Hold your horses, Miss..*

JADE: After a ten-minute interrogation under the guise of small talk, while tens of students come in with their guests no questions asked, we are permitted to enter the accommodation which I pay thousands of pounds to live in.

The plan for the night is going to a formal dinner in the dining hall of the college then Laura wants to go 'out out.' As we have established, there is no 'out out' here and so my actual plan is to get Laura drunk enough that she will want to go to bed. I may have lied to everyone at home that I was having a great time here and the night life popped off. So I couldn't have her finding out the truth.

It takes me so much less time to get ready these days. Quick shower, clothes on and I'm out the door. Laura however...

LAURA: *You can't rush perfection babe. Don't you want me to do your makeup?*

JADE: I reluctantly let her and I put on heels so she doesn't look out of place. This dinner will likely be quite a lot of cardigans and clarks shoes. Plus, if you are a student there, you have to wear a gown over whatever you have on. So I've given up trying to serve any looks.

She's so excited we are literally skipping down the cobbles across the court to the garden room where there's free wine and you mingle before you go in to eat.

As soon as we walk in everyone turns. Laura is acting like it's an episode of 'Kim and Khloe take Miami' and takes my hand and struts towards the wine. And she's off. Chatting to everyone.

LAURA: *Hello Professor. What do u do? You're a eugenicist! Lovely! And what's that then?*

JADE: **Laura, come here NOW. Stop speaking to him he's a freak.**

LAURA: *What dya mean, he's quite fit.*

JADE: **He's a massive racist.**

LAURA: *What? Have yous told the uni?*

JADE: **They know, they gave him a fellowship.**

LAURA: *Why's no one kickin off now? I'll go boot him in the head. Fuckin little Nazi prick.*

JADE: **Laura, stop, please.**

LAURA: *Nah, I won't stop, what's gotten into you?!*

JADE: A professor who teaches on my course is staring at us. I count to five inhaling like what Sue told me to and then I exhale. This is fine. Hermes arrives, followed by Greg who introduces himself by shaking Laura's hand. For fuck sake.

LAURA: *Very formal of you, Gregory. So are you mega rich then or what?*

JADE: Hermes cracks up laughing and the professor comes over.

PROFESSOR: *Are you a member of this college?*

JADE: **You teach one of my papers.**

JADE: He asks who Laura is. I say, this is my sister. He asks if she is my guest. I say yes. He asks if she is an alumni of the university and I say no.

PROFESSOR *Hmm, well, she is going to have to leave and get changed because she is not adhering to the dress code.*

JADE: **What? because her shoulders are out?**

JADE: Hermes asks the professor if he knows what it means to serve cunt.

Laura asks the professor if he's a paedo for shoulders.

Greg asks if any exceptions can be made given he has just been appointed Welfare Officer of the College.

I ask if everyone can please shut up. Then the professor says...

PROFESSOR: *She's drawing too much attention to herself, she will have to leave or we will have to cover her.*

JADE: They bang an ancient gong to signal it's time to head into the dining hall. Greg leaves to answer a phone call from his Dad, who is fuming about his watch and the professor gets a gown and puts it around Laura.

PROFESSOR: *There we go. This is a PHD gown so you get to pretend you have one of those for the evening. Won't that be fun!*

JADE: We walk into the hall in silence. It's huge, like the inside of a castle and everything is candle-lit. The first time I had dinner here I could feel the eyes of the centuries-old paintings judging me. But now their attention was on Laura. We find our places, labelled by hand-written cards like the ones you get at weddings and, as Laura goes to sit, I yank her up from below the elbow. We have to stand and wait behind our chairs until professors and important guests come in last and walk to their seats at the head table at the bottom of the hall.

Another hit of the gong and the Master says grace:

MASTER: *Oculi omnium aspiciunt et in Te sperant, Domine.*

JADE: I had forgot to pre-warn Laura about this bit.

MASTER: *Tu das iis escas illorum tempore opportuno.*

JADE: I'm looking down at the table, feeling like I've swallowed a golf ball.

MASTER: *Aperis Tu manus et imples omne animal benedictione Tua.*

JADE: Laura's silent but I can feel her body shaking. Oh fuck, I've really fucked it.

MASTER: *Benedic nobis, Domine, et omnibus donis Tuis.*

JADE: I should have said something more.

MASTER: *Quae ex larga liberalitate Tua sumpturi sumus.*

JADE: I should have been like: fuck this dinner, fuck the racist prick, fuck the idiot professor, fuck their fucking dresscode, we'll go to Nandos.

MASTER: *Per Dominum nostrum Jesum Christum. Amen.*

JADE: And as I'm about to grab her to leave I can see Hermes, who is in the seat opposite her, making eyes like, like a naughty school kid. He's holding his breath and trying not to laugh and Laura is doing the same.

This IS ridiculous. And I can't believe it has become my new normal. I looked at Laura and I took her hand and whispered 'I'm sorry' and squeeze it tightly until it's over.

JADE: We both went out after in our gowns, and Laura was telling everyone we met that her PHD was in being a bad bitch, before dumping it into the river on our walk home. Greg didn't stay out long cause he wanted to go home to look for his watch again.

Laura left early the next day and I went to Krysyna's kid's birthday at the bowling alley far out of town. I wrapped up my iPad for him because I didn't need it. And it's in my DNA to regift unwanted gifts.

When the party's over and I'm saying bye to Krystyna outside, fucking Tizzo, Tilly Milly and Jilly appear out of nowhere.

TIZZO: *Yooooo, didn't know you were coming today!*

TILLY: *Did Greg invite you?*

JADE: **Nah, I'm just here for... bowling society.**

JADE: Tizzo points to Krystyna as she's driving off.

TIZZO: *Oh, my God, the thief is here!*

JADE: **What?!**

TIZZO: *Haven't you seen Greg's story?*

JADE: I tried to call and he wasn't answering.

I have seven texts from Laura asking directions from King's X to Euston—IT'S ONE STOP GIRL. YOU CAN FIGURE IT OUT.

I cycled back to his college but he wasn't anywhere to be seen.

I get an email from Sue reminding me of two essays I have due with the subject line "Nothing Is Impossible if You Just Believe."

I looked in the common room, in his college bar and even on the footy pitch but I couldn't find him so I went back to my room and even my sea snails looked mad at me.

Krystyna keeps calling me and I keep declining.

I got under my weighted blanket in a desperate attempt to feel sound again.

CLEANER: *You aright, love?*

JADE: My cleaner comes into take my bins out and I realise I don't even know her name.

SCENE 10

JADE: I wake up the next day to my phone ringing. Greg.

JADE: **Why haven't you been replying?**

GREG: *Hey, erm, can you come to my college and see the Dean?*

JADE: Now it took me weeks to figure out that the Dean wasn't just some fella called Dean. The Dean is a person in charge of discipline at each individual college.

DEAN: *Sit down, Jade.*

JADE: Says Dean.
Hermes and Tizzo were already in the room.

DEAN: *Now then. We know you three, as well as the cleaner, are the only people to enter Greg's room in the time his watch has been missing.*

Gregory's father is a significant donor to the university and there will be real consequences if this watch is not found.

JADE: Tizzo asks to be ruled out on cos he is a blood relative, which I dunno cos I would 100% steal a 30k watch from our Laura and cash4gold it. But the Dean nods.

Hermes says that he doesn't need to steal as he is landed gentry, which is a fair point. The Dean nods and looks at me.

DEAN: *And what about you?*

JADE: **He's me fella, why would I rob from me fella?**

HERMES: *She's not a thief just because she's Scouse.*

JADE: The dean nods and accepts my innocence on Hermes' glowing character reference.

TIZZO: *Greg's already told you who took it, this is sooo long.*

JADE: I thought about explaining how I knew it wasn't Krystyna but I've worked too hard to be found out now.

TIZZO: *She always comes in on her ones when I'm asleep, it's sooo bait.*

JADE: And I'm thinkin, the only reason she's doing that is to help me out.

DEAN: *Very well. I will contact the cleaning company this afternoon.*

JADE: **No wait!**

DEAN: *Yes?*

JADE: **I... erm..**

DEAN: *Unless you want to take accountability and face disciplinary action from the university, then I suggest you all get on with your day.*

JADE: I wanted to speak up but I was thinking about the things I'd miss out on. Without this degree I've got nothing, I'd be waving goodbye to my future second home, to my future holidays, to buying my Mum a car. I can't go back to the call centre. Not now I know what a cafetiere is.

So I just stayed quiet.

Krystyna doesn't stop messaging me. She texted again, and again, and I couldn't bring myself to respond. I missed meetings with Sue, and stopped going to lectures. Greg eventually came round to see what was going on with me.

He has flowers and wouldn't leave until I told him what was up. He said I could trust him and that whatever it was he would help.

JADE: **OK, fine, would you still go out with me if I was a sea snail?**

GREG: *Yeah, I love your weird snails.*

JADE: **Would you still go out with me if I could read your every thought?**

GREG: *No way!*

JADE: **Would you still go out with me if I was your cleaner?**

GREG: *Obviously not! Although the boys would think I was a legend if I was fucking my cleaner.*

BIT 3

I'm in the gardens of a Cambridge college in a Vivienne Westwood bridal gown, on what's meant to be the happiest day of my life. None of my family are here because I'm no longer me, I have short nails. With a plain French tip.

I'm indifferent about the things and the people and places I once cared about. I haven't listened to house music in years and I've developed a taste for skiing holidays.

I see Greg and I'm about to marry him.

But instead I run. I run out through the porter's lodge and down the cobbled streets and through the alleyways full of secrets. Like Forrest Gump in a wedding dress. And I keep running.

Sound then. It's time to tell the truth.

JADE: **Look here, Dean. I know I'm in the wrong here, and I am sorry. I didn't know it was a proper rule and if you wanna kick me out cos of it then I understand. I've made me bed, I'll lie in it. Alls I'm saying is, please don't tell the company to sack her because I know she didn't do it.**

JADE: And he literally just believes me. He believes that Krystyna is innocent because I said so, and says he will drop the investigation. My words now hold a power that they didn't once have and I want to cut them up and give them away.

I can hear the Dean telling me how to apply for hardship grants from my college and how they will give me the money to not work and not worry.

The same institution that produces politicians on mass that call mothers tryna feed their kids "benefits scroungers", want to pat themselves on the back for their hardship grants for working class students—when I wouldn't have even heard about them if I wasn't already in shitloads of trouble.

It's like they want people from the 'outside' to come in but then won't let you forget it. You have to be grateful, more grateful than other people because you know they took a chance on you. It wasn't written in the stars of your state education or manifested by your parents round a table in Kensington.

You just got lucky. So stay quiet, and say thank you.

Nah fuck you. Yeno what? I will take your money. And yeno the first thing I'm gonna do? Take our Laura to Nandos. Because we deserve it.

I end up telling Hermes everything. He sits with me while I gather the courage to call Krystyna to tell her why I've been ignoring her.

JADE: **Krystyna... yeah I know about them suspending you. And I'm really sorry I didn't have your back sooner and that I've been ignoring you, I know you didn't do it and...**

JADE: She wasn't calling me cos of the job—as soon as they suspended her she told them to shove it up their arse. She didn't want to work for a place that thought she would do anything like that. She was calling me loads to tell me she'd been accepted onto The Chase. She's absolutely fine.

SCENE 11

JADE: It's time to go home for Christmas. I've dropped off Kyrystna and Tom's prezzies. I call Denise to tell her I'll be back for two weeks. I tell her that I'd only made one friend this term.

DENISE: *"One friend in the storm is worth a thousand friends in sunshine."*

JADE: **Nice one, Denise.**

JADE: I break up with Greg. We weren't compatible, even if he was really fit. Plus I knew that as soon as I hear those four fateful words from a Scouse lad with a head full of turkey teeth...

SCOUSE LAD: *How Are We Girl?*

JADE: ...it would have been game over. Instant adultery. Hermes sends me a voice note:

HERMES: *Have a stunning Christmas, babe. I'm gonna miss you. Next term will be better—I promise. Oh.. and Greg found his watch. It was under his bed.*

JADE: I now have to tackle the biggest issue—London Euston Station. Hell on Earth.

I managed to bag a table seat in coach C—the coach with the onboard shop and excited Hen parties buzzing with Prosecco heading up north for the weekend.

As I'm getting so excited, knowing Laura will be on the platform at Lime Street with something funny on a big sign. I look up and this small but mighty girl, who I recognised from Freshers Fair, the most northern girl I'd ever met, confidently says:

NORTHERN GAL: *Do you mind if sit here?*

JADE: **No, not at all.**

JADE: We got talking and it was like we had been mates for ages. It was like she knew, yeno, like she got it. She was in her third year also doing English, but said she spent most of her time in the theatre writing plays, imagining stuff up and telling stories.

She asked me what my story was, I said:

JADE: **Well, before my life irreversibly changed forever, I worked in a call center. And it was sound but I couldn't shake the feeling that I was destined for much greater things.**

END

ALSO AVAILABLE FROM SALAMANDER STREET

All Salamander Street plays can be bought in bulk at a discount for performance or study. Contact info@salamanderstreet.com to enquire about performance licenses.

A PLAY, A PIE AND A PINT: VOLUME TWO
8 One-Act Plays from Òran Mór.
ISBN: 9781068696237

To celebrate the beloved Glasow theatrical institution's 20th anniversary, this second collection includes critically acclaimed plays and favourites as voted by the public and members of the theatre company.

NOWHERE by Khalid Abdalla
ISBN: 9781068696251

Khalid Abdalla's surprising solo show about his own history and involvement in the Egyptian revolution of 2011.

ATHENS OF THE NORTH
by Mark Hannah
ISBN: 9781068233425

Told across three monologues, the lives of Edinburgh residents and visitors interweave across a single day in Scotland's capital. A love letter tae Edinburgh... past, present... and future.

CARA AND KELLY ARE BEST FRIENDS FOREVER FOR LIFE
by Mojola Akinyemi
ISBN: 9781068233425

Cara and Kelly are best friends, soulmates even. But when a strange new face arrives, unprecedented chaos ensues. Things that once seemed certain are no longer quite so clear. Cara and Kelly, who've never had to doubt each other before, start to question how far they're willing to go for their friendship.